BY THROAT,
BY MIRACLE

BY THROAT,
BY MIRACLE

**Luchadora
Press**

NEW & SELECTED POEMS BY
EDWARD VIDAURRE

Luchadora
Press

Luchadora Press
Copyright © 2023 by Edward Vidaurre
ISBN: 978-1-953447-17-3

Published by Luchadora Press
in the United States of America.

Cover Photo by Edward Vidaurre
Book Layout & Design by Priscilla Celina Suarez

Author Photo by Lonnie Anderson
lonniejanderson.com

Praise for
By Throat, By Miracle

Edward Vidaurre is one of our most uplifting poets and shining spirits. Everything he does is worthy of celebration.

—**Naomi Shihab Nye**, author of *Cast Away: Poems for Our Time* and *The Tiny Journalist*

Edward Vidaurre fills his pen with love and rage and blood. Then he pours in music. And like Jimi Hendrix, when you least expect it, he sets it all on fire as he sacrifices his songs in our honor.

—**Luis Alberto Urrea**, author of *Piedra & Good Night, Irene*

Here he is, the newly crowned Poet Laureate of the Barrio: Vidaurre's poetry is like the fine line of a jail tattoo, the detailed mural on a lowrider car, the jerky slow dance of a cholo. The poems swing to their own beats, yet carry style, color, and breathtaking beauty. ¡Son de acquellas, ese!

—**Luis J. Rodriguez**, author of *Always Running and It Calls You Back*

I love reading and savoring Edward Vidaurre's poetry. *By Throat and By Miracle: New and Selected Poems* shows the earthy as well as the ecstatic range of his poetry. I'm always taken to the borderlands with Vidaurre's poetry, to McAllen, to the Rio Grande Valley, but also to that liminal existence that is the air we breathe in la frontera. I feel I am reading my brother in words, and I can't stop listening to his magic on the page. Bravo.

In his newest collection, *By Throat, By Miracle: New and Selected Poems*, Edward Vidaurre both praises and laments what it has meant to be a child of the barrio—whether tattooed teardrop or stray bullet or the mother's hands that smell of pan dulce. The collection, composed of poems which are exquisitely diverse formally in their use of the page, span selections from eight poetic volumes published in the past decade. The book approaches its conclusion by asking a central question: "what sustains you/ glowing crucifix in the night sky?" ("Moonchrist"), and its more than one hundred poems propel the reader on a quest, and a journey of witness to the concomitant brutality of barrio life and the fierce resilience of the Latinx community. Women figure prominently here as cultural anchors and peace weavers—wives, mothers, sisters, daughters—as moon milk, river stones—love's steadfast, sustaining power despite their wounds. The divine in nature too offers consolation—god as tree, trees as god, or the voice of the Rio Grande whispering. And the poet also turns to literary ancestors—Roque Dalton and "Corky" Gonzales, Cortázar, Lorca, and Ginsberg—as he interweaves languages and tones, moves seamlessly between Spanish and English, between the lyric and the vernacular. These poems howl, they weep, they sing, they prophesy, that is, they carry within them the complex depth of what it means to be human. I have long admired the poems of Edward Vidaurre for their ferocity and tenderness, their precision of craft, and their deep wisdom—they are love in action. *By Throat, By Miracle* is the work of a profoundly wise poet at the height of his artistic power, and he has shown us what it means to live in the skin of another, and to love.

TABLE OF CONTENTS

FROM
CHICANO BLOOD TRANSFUSION

FROM
RAMONA AND RUMI: LOVE IN THE TIME OF OLIGARCHY

FROM
CRY, HOWL

NEW POEMS

ACKNOWLEDGMENTS

I want to thank my publishers Slough Press (*I Took My Barrio on a Road Trip*) El Zarape Press (*Insomnia & Beautiful Scars*), Hercules Publishing (*Love in the Time of Oligarchy*), Prickly Pear Publishing (*JAZzHOUSE* & *Cry, Howl*), FlowerSong Press (*Chicano Blood Transfusion*), & Aztlan Libre Press (*Pandemia & Other Poems*) for believing in my poems.

Also to the literary journals and anthologies that have given individual space to many of these poems. These acceptances gave me courage to continue.

Thank you to the Narciso Martinez Writer's Forum of San Benito, Texas for letting me share my first poem on their stage. To my community of the Rio Grande Valley of south Texas for continued inspiration.

A special thank you to the Texas Institute of Letters who saw me fit to join their distinguished list in 2022.

To the authors that trusted me with their own writings for publication, making me a fan of their souls.

Gratitude and love to Odilia Galván Rodríguez, Priscilla Celina "Lina" Suárez, Rodney Gomez, Carmen Tafolla, Regina Moya, Naomi Shihab Nye, Luis Alberto Urrea, Luis J. Rodriguez, Sergio Troncoso, Robin Davidson, Juan Tejeda, Anisa Onofre, Emmy Pérez, José Antonio Rodríguez, César L. de León, Daniel García Ordaz, Reyes Cárdenas, Victoria Lopez, Lupe Mendez, Vincent Cooper, Jimmy Santiago Baca, Gabriella Gutiérrez y Muhs, everyone at Gemini Ink, and so many of you I hold dear to my heart.

Lilly and Bella, without you nothing is possible, thank you for taking care of my mind, body, and soul through love and sacrifice.

—**Edward Vidaurre**

DEDICATION & MEMORIAM

This book is for my godson and his brother
who left us too soon.

Ruben & Isaiah

In memoriam to the late but ever present Wendy
Barker, Benito Pastoriza Iyodo, Gene Novogrodsky,
& Michael Rothenberg.

INTRODUCTION

Vidaurre's collection *By Throat, By Miracle* took me to mental and emotional extremes, in style, structure, content, making me recall what I had long forgotten—that our Chicano/Latinx culture abounds with magic, that love can be strong as something dropped from fifty storeys high and still walk away, or his case, fly away to the laps and eyes of lonely souls at windows gazing at the stars each night; his poems remind us the Chicano landscape if filled with the most human and epic drama played out each minute-- the barrio's emotional, physical, spiritual essence issue from his mind and heart always inventive, chiseled as water after a thunderstorm, poems swirl, surf, seek, ebb and flow, and at times bring down the mountain of our usual suppositions.

He combines plus and minus images that do not cancel each other out but enhance opposing attributes, attach metaphorical traits to ordinary commonplace items, giving all a refreshing aurora as they display themselves in Chicano mural presentations— he strips, disassembles, rips the veil away of all fashion and pretension and delivers the word without perfume or elite superiority, no indeed-- a linguistic mental conflagration sets to flame whatever his sensibilities happen to touch, consider, mull over.

We assume so much in our ordinary observations, and to that point he obliterates what is normally expected and lavishes the reader with new connections via metaphors, brings together Ginsberg/Kerouac/Whitman, or equally so the surrealists, peeling the surface allure away to expose for us his truer language, a multinational American lexicon, El Chicano language, which reveals a truer cadence and stream of consciousness, an American panoply with black seeds in the pulp and shows us as he guides through his linguistic American culture made of la frontera,

1

Chavez Ravine, it's as if he is conversing with all things rooted in earth while embracing the heart's tendency to destroy and long for, embracing birth and death, hopscotching with purpose, the cosmos with the naïve spirit of a child, clinging to God's hand in a state of mind where God is everything.

—**Jimmy Santiago Baca**, author of *When I Walk Through That Door, I Am an immigrant mother's quest for freedom* and *A Place to Stand*

I TOOK MY BARRIO ON A
ROAD TRIP, 2013

SUMMER IN EL SALVADOR

They made us pull to the side of the road
rifles pointed, one on me and one on my tío

"Hijo! No hables, no digas que vienes del otro lado."

The two soldados circled the VW microbus
loaded with University textbooks
to be delivered to "La U" in San Salvador

I looked at my shoes and my heart sank
brand new high tops, they don't even sell
these here, me entró el miedo

As they got closer I didn't know whether to smile,
frown, look away or what
but I could see the struggle in their eyes
jovencitos about the age of my older brother
dieciocho o diecinueve por ay'

Ragged in camouflage
tough and threatening
sweat trickling
the nervous kind
The kind that pools on the upper lip
and beads the forehead

They jumped into the backseat of the
Volkswagen minivan and pointing the tip of the
rifle ordered my uncle to drive until he said when to stop
his voice cracked, like his man voice was just developing and he
knew it, so the bullets clicking into the rusty weapon put hair on
his chest

We drove with a faint sound the busted speakers let out
a song by Alvaro Torres, for a while we all listened
then they laughed, and lit up some cigarettes

At a distance I could see the coffee plantation
the aroma was comforting
as warm urine spread all along
the seat of my pants and down my leg

That drive of about six kilometers
felt like it took all day
I saw the most beautiful sunset disappear
behind the dark green mountains over
Lake Coatepeque

BARRIO NIGHT

He looks in the mirror, a tattooed teardrop & permanent frown
mark his face

Smoke billows around
the room as thoughts surface

Flashbacks
at the speed of light engulf him

Running with his little sister around their flat
  -a barking dog
  -balloons
  -piñatas
  -a backyard BBQ

His first crush, sweet
Soft and a wet sensation
of young love develop

Shooting up carga
drinking and dancing
barrio oldies in slow circles with
her full breasts pressing against his muscular chest with the
letters FTW in old English letters carved sloppily

Cruisin'
boulevard nights
the sun sets over the First Street Bridge

It all came back
in that split second

The smoke around the room
a burning cigarette on the edge of
the sink & the noise
of a bullet cap
were the only witnesses

to the tear trickling
alongside his temple

tonight... a toe tag
& a whisper in the night
will go unheard on this cold
barrio night

THE BULLET OF '91

A bullet
came knocking on
my door tonight

I opened and noticed
the worn metal
reddish brown,
tired, &
-winded

I asked it to come inside
& poured us some coffee

it asked if I was from Aliso Village
"yes" I responded

it broke down and gunpowder
clouded my vision
never seen a bullet cry before,
It spoke, telling me
that he was intended for
my heart since 1991 &
has been taking lives ever since

he says he's traveled through many barrios,
shot out through car windows,
up in the air, even small distances as close as a few inches

but that it was my turn,
gritting its metal teeth and made an angry face

I picked it up and brought it to my lips
kissed it
& forgave it

POETIC DRIVE-BY

dandelions
blowing seeds
near the rose bushes along the wall
sprayed with bullet holes from the night before

the dampness in July
giving moisture to my garden
is of his blood

it was a clear night
oldies played in the background
Jaime smiled as he opened the cap from his 40
it was a good day overall

the sun set
and his mistake
was to give this barrio a chance

the prelude to the ghetto birds shine
was inevitable. The siren lights
from the police car were polished,
the yellow tape had been ordered
and put in the trunk, the police officer
would go home later that night and
hold his daughter tight.

Her cries, would haunt him for life

The vato got a haircut and the scent of
tres flores trailed with the breeze

before he could write about candlelit nights with
you by his side, drinking red wine, slow dancing,
and whispering "I love you's"
sharing dreams and traditions
the bullet would pierce through
his hands, spilling ink
in a daze -her lips mouthing

"Te amo"
While caressing his head

they caught the culprit before
the chalk outline was traced over his hands

a poet died, pobre vato
a blank page was read at his wake

THE NIGHT PERFECT DIED

I remember you
you were across the room,
I sipped on a chela listening to a song
by Ralfi Pagan

We looked at each other and it was perfect
you liked my creased pants and batted your eyelashes
I liked your feathered hair and you stared at me
looked over to your girlfriend and she giggled

she got up, walked away
nodded for me to come sit next to you

we sat in silence
I tried to speak and so did you
I waited for you
you did too

you smelled
pretty
my hands were sweating and then
Smokey came on the record player

I reached over
took you by the hand
we stood up
I put my hands around your waist,
yours on my shoulders
I could see the freckles behind
your heavy makeup and
a small mole above your lip

a bala vaga
pierced through the wall
and tore my perfect flower in two

I fell in love
You fell to the floor

nights when I'm alone, I remember
your trembling hand
your smell
your smoky eyes

Your lips
the ones
I never kissed
trembled, then stopped

LOS TENDEDEROS

Most of my friends had sisters, hermanas
I would hang out with them in los tendederos

A long stretch of cable from one post to another
My mom would tell me to take the wet clothes and
Hang them to dry, I clipped the clothes pins
Yo the edge of my tshirt and one by one hung our
Chonies, socks, jeans, and sabanas to dry

The prettiest girls never talked
En los tendederos, the mothers always
Asked questions like, "donde esta tu mama?"
Or say things like, "te vi el otro dia con esa bola de cabroncitos"
Then follow up with advice and how their kids were
The perfect example, but really weren't

Sometimes it would rain, sometimes clothes
Would go missing. I would see my shirt on
The local hobo the next day, sometimes
It was my favorite shirt.

Sometimes I miss the exchanges
In los tendederos, the way the sheets would
Dance with the breeze, and the girls would
Tip-e-toe to get the last of the bed sheets to stay,
Or the chisme and complaints from the lady
That never left her home except to dry her clothes

Sometimes the clothes would stay overnight

FOTO NOVELAS

Boxes and bags full of
El Libro Semanal
Were traded between comadres
Las vecinas and my mom would
Sit and read these little books
Where the women were drawn
To look like goddesses and the
Chiseled bodies on men brought out
Long sighs in women, funny what
A drawing can do with a little caption
Of what a man would say to a woman
To woo her

I read them and learned to write
In Spanish, I learned what women
Wanted from men to romance them.

But I was a kid, and forgot about
It all when I had my first brush with
Sweaty palms and butterflies in my stomach,
My first crush.

Her name was Lupita.
And all I wanted to do was
Hold her hand and stare at the scar over her eye

I TOOK MY BARRIO ON A ROAD TRIP

for three days

everywhere I went   there it was

my barrio

there were times I had to put it in my pocket

-mi barrio

but out it came from my lips

I took my barrio on a road trip
to Austin

together we stood
side by side

together
we ate, drank, and smoked

no matter where I tried
telling my barrio to stay
it followed me

protecting me, giving me advice

"get a hold of yourself" it would tell me
"you can do this ese!"
"no te rajes!"

I took my barrio on a road trip and from now on
I will take it with me everywhere I go

WOUNDS OF A WOMAN

She stands behind promises, hope, and love

Enter the wound "Abortion"

womb in pain
but the sex was good
child erased

His whispers were calming
torn soul
the boy smelled right
she hugs her pillow
as she drifts to the day she died a little
along with baby drool she will never see
and murdered fairies with fractured glass slippers

The wound of "Rape"

Her mind and brain spin
out of control
she hears her clothes being torn
as her nails dig for his face to disappear
her blood and his
stain the air around them and the sheets below them lost forever
between
his world and hers
she screams into nothing

The unforgiving wound of "Incest"

The wound that owns the whispers of life
and the endless tears no one wants to see

he was her prince
her little hands then, and now
twenty years later
tremble
still crying herself to sleep
in a whispered tone saying
"Daddy! Why? Why, My daddy?
The wounds from the "Beat-down"

"Shut your damn mouth!"
the words before the blow
a new mark to make up for the healing rainbows
across her body

Even at night they adorn her face
blanketing her almond-shaped eyes
her jaw locks
she prefers to stay silent

The wound of "Self-Esteem"

She starves herself
close to the bone
her hips barely hold her skirt
while she flips through the pages of the Cosmo
telling her, "you can't be loved unless...?

The final wound "Suicide"

fumbling through her messy world
in search of hope
just dead-ends greet her
birds have gone mute
music is silent
colors dull
on the restroom floor
Paracetamol pills tic-tac-toe across
the tile as she takes her last gasp

seeing hope, she reaches out
a bit too late, she slips into the darkness
where light is no more

FROM

INSOMNIA, 2014

SUBMERGED

Let me finish this poem before you disappear
into the India ink across my chest.

I only dream of you
on nights when
the sullen fog drifts
into the broken wood bridge near the resaca where my
body appeared to
the barefoot children
de mi colonia

Sirena sumergida,
las aguas lloran por ti las aguas lloran por ti

Everything you do,
you do in secret,
you think in code,
and speak in murmurs yet,
when you speak of love it's loud and clear
for my heart
and that is enough
for me

that is enough for me

en tus ojos descanso,
en tus ojos descanso... hundido

RESACA DREAMS

This poem is accompanied
by a slow strumming guitar

sung by the many voices
lost in the prodigal whispers

of mort—the piety of the poor,
the cachinnation of border town

children, the wisdom of the viejitas
y viejitos, and, finally . . . by the moon

that painfully shines a light on my greatest
fear: a floating love that wished to be a mermaid

instead morphing into a catán.

note: a catán is an alligator gar—a large, toothy, freshwater fish

PANTOUM DREAM

I will dream of ancient rains that fall
drop by drop
beat by beat
from the blood-red skies

drop by drop
from the faucet of humanity
from the blood-red skies
the souls of purgatory will cry

from the faucet of humanity
saints will wander,
the souls of purgatory will cry
lost in nostalgic dreams

saints will wander,
amongst the daydreamers,
lost in nostalgic dreams
breathing towards a vanishing afterlife

amongst the daydreamers,
side-by-side with forgotten lovers,
breathing towards a vanishing afterlife
my heart slows down

side-by-side with forgotten lovers,
poems become hymns and
my heart slows down
diminished

poems become hymns and

watch the lonely moon drown in the black waters below— diminished, forgotten and in love—
alone.

AT YOUR FRONT DOOR

You live out in the middle of nowhere. The doorbell rings. It's five past midnight. The dog pants and the oak tree out front brings its leaves to a hush. The cookie dips into the ice cream slowly. You try to quiet your breathing. There's a knock this time. The phone rings. Your heart stops. The door opens. The dog runs. You fade.

IN A BRIEF INSTANCE. SHE VANISHED...
LIKE A WHISPERED KISS ON THE FINGERTIPS

Like a northern wind disturbing
an afternoon siesta
              making me forget
the end of the dream

Like a peripheral vision
        of great grandma holding her
heart, strung to a star
                    leaving drops of blood
for the stray cat to lick

Like a hobo smacking his lips
after a swig of rawness
            killing what's left of his dignity

Like pennies in a wishing well
            drowning a child trying to steal
its riches

Like the creepy fog that gossips from
town to town
            in search of
a wailing woman
            with bite marks
on her ankles.

NIGHT

I'm writing in the dark.
The exhaled smoke makes creepy images that dance into this bitch
of a night.

I'm writing in the dark.
The mosquitoes line up.
I see them take flight towards me as they die tonight.

This bitch night—
pale,
still—
hot mess of a night.

I LOST MY SOUL IN THE RIVER STYX
THAT FLOWS FROM BETWEEN YOUR THIGHS

I'll call that agony of space
Phlegethon,

where I will wade my hands
on the side of each tower
upward into the ecstasy
of your sheath.

I lost my soul
exploring the
passage of humanity,

plunging into
experience. Like Thetis,
be my mother and dip me
into the darkness of your
hungry river.

Are you Charon?
What or how much
do I owe you?

When will you swallow me?

FRAGMENTS

Last night I dreamed about you. You left your lips on my pillow and toes on the dresser, you left your shoes under the bed and your earrings in my mouth, you left your hands on my chest and thighs on the chair in the corner, you left your breath on my neck and ring in my hand. Your breasts are still on top of the radio, and your eyes . . .

well, your eyes . . .

I'm wearing them.

CONVERSATION WITH MY GREÑUDA

What do I write for?

To make sense of how fast my daughter is growing and how I'm
slowing down.
She disappears into the blues, yellows, greens and tans of the
playground asking what the syringe on the floor is used for.

I tell her it's the sadness of what's left from last night's rain. I tell
her it's what's left of a fight between life and death. I tell her
It's what's left.

She tells me
she thinks it's what keeps kids playing indoors,
building imaginary castles
and molding their future
with Play-Doh.

Though it makes no sense, she makes sense of it:
evil lurks, and if you're not right
wrong is magnified,
leading you to the edge between reason and insanity.

"Why is the playground empty?"
she asks.
I say it's because kids don't know how to play.

She says, "Or maybe parents need to be led by their hands and not
be afraid to get grass stains on their skinny jeans." (There I knew
she wasn't speaking about me.)

I say it may be true.

She says, "I'm glad you're my dad."
I say, "I'm glad you love swings and slides."

She smiles.

UNWINDING

To my left
Erotic stories
To my right
A naked woman
In front of me
A poem with illustration

ANOTHER NIGHT

I shook in my sheets
the barrio stirred
dogs barked
doors opened
people spoke
the moon gave light
parents counted heads
two blocks down
one went uncounted
the news came fast
a mother's heart ached
she tore through the yellow tape
mouth wide open
screaming into the dead night
without a sound
another night
in my barrio
the silence is at times
too loud
to handle

sometimes

at night

GINSBERG SHEETS

Ginsberg sheets
soiled by the men
of a thousand kisses deep

Howling
for the Muses
to wake
to join in our insomnia

Restless nights
of blue midnight
sadness, waking up
to a somber jazz tune.
In the distance
where shadows have
lost their owners
to last night's suicide

I lie in Ginsberg's
sheets, soiled
by men with needle
tracks on their toes,
sitting next to windows,
looking out into
the third dimension
searching for zombie
hipsters in high-top sneakers.

I fall off,
counting the flights
until I reach your street,

splattering poems,
bleeding ink.

My toe tag reads:
UNKNOWN BEAT.

MIDNIGHT BLUE

If I played the harmonica, the sound would be of midnight blues,
tattooed tears running down the face of God, of heroin blasts
through unpainted canvases, a shrill of a deep shank into the
breast of Mother Earth, the ripping from the roots of fruit trees
being yanked from the concrete jungles of America's ghettos.
If I played the harmonica—and played it well—the poor would
hunger no more, and poetry would serve its purpose.

FROM

BEAUTIFUL SCARS: ELEGIAC BEAT POEMS, 2015

BEAUTIFUL SCARS

When we met, she worried about the scars. Asked that I close my eyes forever if I wanted to love her for just as long . . . deep beautiful scars that pierced through her like a falsetto. White lines that resembled rivers across the sky—contrails. Years of anguish broke the surface of her skin. When I arrived, I thought I could heal them . . . I thought I was the one to mend, be a salve. The scars are now on me. Now it's her turn to close her eyes forever . . . give me a shot at this thing called love.

SKIN OF YOUR TEARS

(After José José's "Almohada")

I've been sifting through the dead skin you left behind on your pillow for the past two nights. Your scent is all but gone. A lone hair tangles itself on my fingers. The tear stains never dried. I will lay here with a view of a street that saw you drive off to the south as my prayers took off into the unforgiving night. I heard your voice cry out. Got up to look. . . . nothing there but a pair of mismatched stiletto heels, one with a torn strap, the other with a scuff mark. I turned off the lights about three minutes past one in the morning. . . . Next to me, your scent returned to reclaim its layer of skin that fell off your shadow, leaving me alone with your tears that take up your side of the bed.

SLEEPING THROUGH THE SMOKE

I read some Rumi before bed and in the dream I was on my way to a
Bed & Breakfast but never left town due to some odd circumstance.
I smoked several cigarettes in my dream as I sat on the ledge of a
high-rise apartment complex. As I got up, I walked down the open air
staircase. I passed indigenous families talking in their native Nawat.
I understood them but could not answer back. They would just
say, "He's the poet who almost jumped. It seems he still loves her."

*Pipil (Nawat in the native tongue) is an ancient language spoken
in Central America, similar to the ancient Aztec Náhuatl.

POLYSYNDETON RIOT

I remember my mom telling me to run over anyone who got in my way during the L.A. Riots as I made my way through South Central to pick her up from work. My 1970 Buick Skylark had a full tank of gas. I prayed the sniper's stray bullet wouldn't hit my gas tank. I was ready to flatten bodies, and it was in April of 1992, and I was nineteen, and I was scared, and I didn't loot, and I played Ice Cube, and they did "Burn That Motherfucker Down!"

SOME DAYS

not even music does it. Chocolate ice cream doesn't do it. She
sits looking at old photographs in silence. The kind of place that
does it serves hot tea instead of coffee. I love coffee. Hold the
pen knowing the blank page is perfect. Days play out. My favorite
chair is uncomfortable. I move. The rain is perfect; she sleeps
through it. Its loudness cripples me; meanwhile she looks for
that pill fix. Bliss is catching the last fly in the room after we've
destroyed the air around us. It's never too late to begin a life of
love. The dancing hula girl on her dashboard: I want to stop it.
The lone penny left on the hot asphalt outside a gas station: I
want to pick it up. The marker with a missing top causing it to
go dry: I want to cover it because it just makes things better. Is
it a better world? Maybe so. Then we hear of 150 people being
vaporized on the side of a mountain and we feel like shit. That's
when I set my alarm and count sheep— count them one by
bloody one. Some days, not even music does it. Even my shadow
walks faster than me.

CHIAROSCURO

Somewhere between the shadows that walk during our sleep paralysis, there's a song. It has no color, veiled like a procession of widows on their way to visit their handsome dead. It strums and strings along, never giving itself in absolution to sorrow . . . instead walking, and singing a new song of hope—a bright tune.

TELLING THE BEES

I'll knock on the beehive that hangs outside your house, near
the tree that hides stories of a noose that silenced every leaf this
summer. I'm telling the bees. I'm telling them about the day
comedy committed suicide and every depressed person walked
the streets in procession, pouring their sadness into the gutters
that also washed away the dark crimson from Eric Garner's
neck, from Emmett Till's eyes, from Octavio Rojas Hernandez's
journals, from my dad's vomit into the eyes of cancer.

I'm telling the bees of your departure into the arms of the
trumpet's wail, of your heart's mischief with the decorated hero's
tainted star, and the riffs of the cover band's mute guitar strings.

I'm telling the bees. I'm whispering. I'm singing it to them. I'm
telling them . . . interrupting them, as they sting me one by one.
I'll make them listen to me.

I'm telling the bees. I'm telling the bees, gently, but I'm telling
them . . . that when you return, just walk right in. I'll be
producing honey on the back porch. I'll be making it sweet—
producing a fresh batch of . . .

Welcome home, My Love.

OUR LAMENT

dad.
tears.
dad. more. tears.
dad.
love.

ELOY, THE LION

I.

. . . and when I get the news of your passing, the sun will emerge with liver spots that will cast shades on the earth. People will fight for the parking spots where there is no shine because leather seats after hours in the sun . . . well, burn. Your shadow will walk away into the fragments of the morning fog. The moon will understand. I've told her about you many times. She will weep into the ocean and curse the highest mountain with darkness. Church bells will ring and incense will burn for you. I will think too much about it and dig up every worm in my backyard and chew on it. I will want to know everything about you, a bit late. You never knew much about my poetry, but it's okay because now you're my new poetry. I will keep you alive and your hair will continue to grow. I'm glad you had a ridiculously handsome laugh. Even when you tried being mean, you were tender in the eyes.

Take the color blue with you, like the uniforms of many years of hard work. Take with you all the gold, like the ring with the peridot stone. Take the color yellow as well and hand it to my biological father and tell him not to be jealous, but thankful. Maybe you can sneak a lock of Mother's hair into heaven, put it at the feet of Mary, and walk away in silence. She will know. Take 10 degrees of heat and toss it into St. Jude's garden. This cancer thing, leave it behind: let us figure it out. Look into the mirror before you go. Stand up straight and see my reflection, the face of your three beautiful girls and two other boys, your grandchildren too. You did good, Pop. Feel the breath of your wife on your face and her soft hands in yours.

My daughter asked, "Is he my last grandpa?". . . I said "Yes."

She cried.

I cried.
I explained.
She understood.

She ran off to draw and color a picture in pinks, blues and yellows with ribbons and tears. I told her to draw an avocado.

She asked after the drawing was complete, "What is going to happen to him?"

I told her, "He will be a new season, a mix between spring and summer, a dash of winter and a chunk of fall."

II.

In heaven, he is on the radar: INCOMING:
"Eloy, the Lion!"

THE MOON

is the most beautiful I've seen since I stopped taking her for granted.
People are coming out of taverns and apartment complexes, two-
story homes and trailer parks to see. They're pulling over to gawk
at her in the total darkness of the Petrified Forest on Route 66. But
she belongs to me tonight, and I will not share her. She showed
me her nakedness at noon, while others were too busy to notice.
She's slimmer than usual in her fullness. I noticed. She's reading
my poems on her reflection in the sea.

CHAOS

Her mouth
d
r
o
p
s

vacant lyrics into
an empty glass

perhaps
it's a howl

perhaps
it's an echo

perhaps
it's a murmur

LATELY,

love tastes like broken English, feels like jive talk, sounds like the
water that sloshes under the pier as you look over the madera at a
close distance to the cotton candy. It feels like a cat searching for
a warm engine in the winter. Amor ahogado, sin ganas, distracted,
overdosing on false hope and kind words from poets that hide
behind sonnets and suede shoes. Lately, love is *like,* and *like* is not
enough. Love needs suero, a drip bag of aguántate un poco mas.
But I'll wait for a transplant—wait for a donor. And somewhere out
there, soon, someone will die of heartache and maybe, just maybe,
the donor and I will be a match.

FALL IN LOVE ON DAYS

when the weather outside coincides with the season. When gas is less by the gallon than the week before. Fall in love when the milk in the fridge expires. When a Big Mac tastes like heaven. Fall in love on frigid days that allow for reading a mystery novel. Fall in love to the sound of a distant trumpet. When poems speak to you— or don't. Fall in love when you accept your fat. Fall in love when you have a month to live. Love on Mondays. Fall in love during the season finale. Love because hating hurts. Fall in love with her eyes, her lips, her voice, her off-key singing. Fall in love in the shower, up on the roof, behind the bleachers. Fall in love in November. Count her freckles. Erase her sadness. Fill her empty arms. Love her farts. Fall in love with her funny toe. Love her madly.

LLUVIA

Outside it rained—

A desperate downpour

relámpagos contra su reflexión

afuera—llueve
sin cesar

adentro se ahoga

END OF CONVERSATION

We speak through beads of sweat, through dust particles that are prevalent just as the sun starts its descent into the thirsty ocean. We speak after six, again just before dinner—when the home smells of chicken broth, and just before the last of the cilantro sprigs's backstroke. We speak late, her hands tucked under the pillow. I speak with my hands caressing her back. My hands—the ones that memorized each curve and, like a blind man reading Braille, can read each of her scars with my eyes closed. Her mouth opens to speak, but the breaths—against my skin—are lacerations that say it all. We've said it best by saying nothing at all.

CHICANO BLOOD
TRANSFUSION, 2016

LOS DESAPARECIDOS

Perseus with the head of Medusa (Mujer Zeta decapitada por el Cartel del Golfo) Oil on linen 7ft tall by 5 1/2 feet wide. 2014 by Rigoberto A. Gonzalez

Everyone has the gift of invisibility,
even the border wall goes unnoticed in June after a
month that drains us of life. The scent of knives
on a hot summer is the only constant
amongst the news of frontera tragedies and a poetry
reading in a stick-to-your-skin humid bar in a small South Texas town.

We all have the gift of going missing,
like the breath of a collapsing lung,
like a whisper from behind, a shooting star.
Or do we just hide reading a newspaper upside-down
when the new Sheriff arrives?

Puede ser que también los periódicos se convierten
lanchas que se lanzan en un río olvidado, en aguas
color a sangre de tantos que casi por las yemas de los dedos
tocaban tierra Estadounidense.

The missing,
they recite Howl across the Rio Grande
but not the Ginsberg lament for his brethren
but the howls of suffering souls crammed in stash houses
 across our children's playgrounds, those left
for dead in sweltering sardine packed vessels,
-those left alive to remember hell is real.

Los desaparecidos,
quieren ser encontrados
aún decapacitados y sin lenguas.

Siguen gritando porque el silencio es fuerte en sufrimiento.

We will keep them alive and find them!
Through art, poetry, music, stories that scare the night,
and lullabies that make our children sleep tight.

Cuando los cantos se vuelven agua
el olor de cuchillos en el aire
bailan con la bougainvillea trepadora
descendiendo seis pies bajo la tierra sin nombre
-solo una alabanza que fluye entre la tierra agrietada

*cuando los cantos se vuelven agua: Martín Espada-gracias por la
inspiración*

HERMANO

Leaves on the retama
have been gone for a while now
as has my brother, who left behind

his pants on the mesquite
branches just under
la baya de muérdago y anacua.

Where did you go, hermano?

Was it you who ate from
the prickly pear? Was it your blood
I saw on the concrete slab
near the cattle crossing beyond
the chaparral? Did you

drink from the sultry air
when you got thirsty
and the hunger pangs set in?

I'll be back soon, leave me
your water bottles, even if
empty.

STRAY BULLET #3

Corridos play,

en la cocina
Mamá stirs el caldo

en la sala
la más chiquita falls into
her tea set: she serves

blood to her dolls.

LORCA IN THE BARRIO
(ode to Lorca's Fable and Round of the Three Friends)

Travieso,
Chepe,
Lalo

the three of them frozen:
Travieso by the world of bullets;
Chepe by the world of syringes and acid trips;
Lalo by the marching of monks through his barrio.

Travieso,
Chepe,
Lalo

the three of them burned:
Travieso by the world of pigeon shit and chalk outlines;
Chepe by the world of drive by shootings and rucas with feathered hair;
Lalo by the world of banned literature and dead lecturers.

Travieso,

Chepe,
Lalo,
the three of them buried:
Travieso in Lupitas tattoo;
Chepe in the carga going through his bloodstream:
Lalo in the roosters crow, the dog's howl, and the glossy eyes
of his tecato father.

Lalo,
Chepe,
Travieso,

the three in my hands were
three Zoot Suit scholars,
three crooked cops,
three birds of different races and a Autumn spirits
that flew around landing in blood stained sidewalks being
outlined by death.

Uno

y uno
y uno,
los tres enterrados,
con la ternura del Invierno,
con la tinta negra de palabras escritas antes del suicido de la
Primavera,
con las lágrimas de Sofía que espera ser realidad en el útero del
Verano,
por la miel que llora la Luna hace el triste
     mar en Otoño.

Three

y dos
y uno,
I saw them run, hide and die
on the streets of Los Angeles
into a dark alley,
into the night of anxiety filled smog,
into the voiceless screams and anguish of their mother's
    open mouths.
into my sadness of domestic abuse and alcoholism,

into the bar with the velvet curtain,
into my own death unannounced last year.

I killed the last of the Chicano writers
and a few people in Arizona held their champagne flutes in the
air.

While Menchita tucked in their little wonderful children to the
tune of
La llorona, breathing over them.
Travieso,
Chepe,
Lalo.

Chicanas are hard,
but sometimes if you lay your head,
between their soft breasts you can hear the cries of a new
generation
of raza with the knowledge and power to make a man shit in fear,
y eso me conforma

Cuando ya no pude ver las luces de la ambulancia
pasando la loma sobre la calle Cesar Chavez
entendi que me asesinaron también a mi.
Esa noche en el barrio destaparon todas las sábanas blancas
buscándome entre las caras fallecidas, en las iglesias, los
panteones,
callejones, y las aguas del río frío.
Still they couldn't find me.
No pudieron?
No they couldn't.

Sin balas en mi cuete,
pero con un libro y lápiz en mi mano,
empece a escribir poemas...

VALLEY GIRL

She's a WiFi hotspot,
a real page turner,
lips with erotic stories,
a beauty on the outer edges
of my retina, soft
-a diva

She's happily ever after
Fantasies carved out of mesquite
With sunflower hair,
Chasing dreams on the back
Of a javelina
-near resacas

She's pucker lipped,
Red dawn toughness,
Boot strapped,
Scuff marks tattooed on her
Breasts that heave
-with the sound of accordions

She's downtown,
Corner street,
Red light special
A fishnet stocking mess
-tumblin' out of Lopez bar
With lipstick smeared
By who knows who

She's chilaquiles
After midnight
Triangle cut

-corn tortillas
 hot and melted
Over the top

She's country
Jeans, beer, gum chewing
Mollcjas dorada,
Chamoyada y raspas
White wing shooter
-a Valley girl

DOWN THE LINE

Swinging at bruised leather baseballs and trying to keep it between second and third base. Barrio rules. We were latch-key kids living near four miles south of Dodger Stadium, or, as the older *veteranos* in the neighborhood called it, Chavez Ravine. They claim the *gobierno* came down on the landowners who were Mexican-American and took their *pedazo* of the American Dream. Why? I don't know, but it never stopped them from wearing blue-and-white *"doyer"* caps and being proud when *"Fernandomania"* took the baseball world by storm.

You already knew who would win, who would hope to win, and who would struggle. *Chepito* would struggle most. He bent and hunched over the plate and always swung late, making sure the ball would go foul or down the line in the wrong direction. These were the rules plain and simple. For *Chepito* the game was hard and complicated. Then there was Juan, square-jawed, muscular: *"el mero mero honronero."* His brothers were all athletes—even his beautiful sister, Maria could outrun us. We would all pause and wait to see how far he could hit the ball. All the *chavalitos* would run past the center-fielder—back, back, back where it would be gone.

The bully gang-bangers rode around in "borrowed" bicycles with cigarettes hanging from their lips as the stillness of summer allowed for an inch of ash to hang from their pubescent hairline mustaches. The girls sat at a distance while the boys glanced over, trying to hit the ball into the gap at left-center, showing off, yelling loudly with their off-key mini machismo selves. I sat watching the *homies* making memories in my mind, sipping on a cream soda until it was my turn to bat. We played hard and tattooed sweat marks on our t-shirts, making spider web designs across our backs. Some of us had plastic gloves with half our hands sticking out and some had the leather mitts that were passed down from their older siblings with spit stains, and—if they were lucky—a Steve Garvey autograph.

If you hit the ball between right-center it would carry towards the cafeteria of the school grounds where we played after the last employee left for the day. Not too far from where I tasted my first kiss from Chicana lips, moist and strange—her tongue confused me into manhood, making me *firme* after rounding second with the prettiest girl I knew.

Down the line, down the streets, *curvas* thrown at us—life always trying to count us out. We played until the first call from our mothers rang through the barrio, until the sun abandoned us, until the gunshots sounded, or until Vin Scully's voice was tuned down on the television to listen to the radio broadcast of Jaime Jarrin's voice translating the game known to us as *beisbol*.

BEAT-ROTICA

Your hair is soft
soft and splendid   sometimes i wish there was no God   to
know all my thoughts
to know of my thoughts   the things i would do to you   the nerve of me
selfish   self taught in the ways of sinful pleasures   i want to
learn them with you
i want to forget about the moon with you   the moon frowns and
the stars die

it was the brick and post   it was walking fast past the voodoo shops
it was the chicory   it was the jazz   it was fifty two degrees   it was
definitely the jazz

it had to be the jazz
it was the voodoo we found in the alley   underneath the
emergency staircase
it was the lipstick smeared on my chest   the things i would do to you

splendid like the face of death   right before the orgasm of our shadows
like the orgasm of hollywood and vine   the nerve of me
again the moon shines   and again it dies   again we forget

it was the palm trees swaying
it was the open mouth of the coming sea
it was the sun
it was poetry
it was smoggy and overcast
it was definitely the poetry
it had to be the words
it was the kiss from your lips `
the hard on you left behind   on them boys
their imagination   of your lips   on what you left behind

again the moon rises   and dies   and is forgotten   the stars die
it was this poem
erotic and selfish   turning heads   giving blowjobs in the rain
it was your lips   falling from the sky gasping to die before the land
slowly praying before it lands
on the pages
of time

we sit across from each other
with the grains in our mouths
of coffee from the french press
waiting for the first word
to come out of our filthy mouths

a song of sadness   a song of sexual intercourse   of course
a song of sex   a song that will die   along with the moon and the stars

CHICANO BLOOD-TRANSFUSION

I got shot in the gut
and now I need
a Chicano blood transfusion.

Make sure the vials come from the underground.

Quick!

alurista is coming down the corridor and wants my hat for his
collection

What for the rush and bloody pain
What for the blooming and the rain

Close the door! Put a sheet over my body and tag my toe.
My brown skin is hindered by the loss of blood.

Help! Minute men are looking for me,
la migra is banging on my door!
La chota has me surrounded
In hand, pistolas with hairline triggers,

I can hear them approaching with
their steel- toed boots crushing
the concrete up the piss stained staircase.
breaking out the chalk, ready to outline me
for being a Voice

Where's the sangre?
I'm losing consciousness
strap Juan Felipe Herrera down

-take it from him
cause' I can only come up with 180 reasons why a Guanaco can't
cross the border.

Look for the descendants of
"Corky" Gonzales

*who also is the blood,
the image of myself.*

 Ask a Chicana in the midst
with beautiful brown eyes,
to hold my hand during the
mezcla of Pupil y Maya

I can't write anymore, my pen is missing
along with my grandma's recipe for champurrado y chiles
rellenos.

I need those to help me break
through the concrete wall mierda stretching from Califas to Tejas.

I worry about my citizenship/permiso para jalar/needing a
haircut on Sundays
 I worry about people that drive small cars/con placas vencidas/
con placas behind them

STOP!

Alright I think it's done
I feel the same

Chingón!
Guanaco!
Chicano!
Angeleno!

Tejano!

With the blood of
Mi gente del barrio

CHOLO

"Sometimes the barrio claims us, holds us by our feet like roots in its field of chalk outlines closed off by the screaming yellow tape being pulled from its soul."

There's a cholo in my poems
he wanders and peeks his head in and out
of each stanza

He is walking the straight lines
in my journals
drawing caskets, spray painting the edges,
kissing my girl and making his saliva
drain down her throat
bypassing her heart,
flowing down,
carving his initials in her insides

He lives deep inside
finds corners of her heart
where tears well up before they make
their way out.
He sits with his head down, cap pulled back,
smoking on a cigarette, taking slow drags
blowing heart-shaped smoke rings
towards her baby blue lungs

He runs fast inside of me
pushing through my guts
piercing like a stray bullet.

He skips over pages of my life
written in red ink

inhaling paint fumes through paper bags,
in worn out shoes, mind on his money,
revenge and crying with thoughts of his
madrecita

This cholo reads books,
chews up his fingernails
-spitting into the mulch that covers
the syringes in the playground where
his little sister was kidnapped, and found
days later roaming,
listless, confused, but alive

He sits
on my front porch
with beer cans at his feet
near the puddle of piss
and burnt out joints

he enjoys haikus
that remind him of his love,
summer, acid trips, and sex

He's a cholo
who wanders and intertwines.
Like a pantoum of veins in my stomach
he caresses my soul

Who wanders and intertwines.
Between life and death
he caresses my soul
leaving me for dead.

RAMONA AND RUMI: LOVE IN
THE TIME OF OLIGARCHY, 2018

IN SEARCH FOR THE SADDEST SONG

rumi leaves early in the morning
Searching for the saddest song
He walks over to the river
He hears birds sing
Perched above
A tree

A tree
Sad, looming
He hears birds sing
He walks over to the river
Searching for the saddest song
Rumi returns late in the afternoon

Ramona puts out her hand for rumi
To hand over the melancholic lyric
He brought it from the river
Where birds sing, sadly
The saddest song
A long cry

A long cry
The saddest song
Sad songs the birds sang
From over by the rio grande river
A lyric so sad and melancholic both cried
Ramona and rumi cried into each other hands

Ramona and rumi cried along the river of El Rio Grande
After listening to the saddest song the birds sang
Perched above, sad on the anacua tree
Then they slowly came to a hush
The saddest song
A body

A body
A song on replay
Slowly rising from the waters
A small child, a belt, no shoes, one sock
All the birds flee, carrying with them the saddest song

IMMIGRANT DINNER

rumi prepares accidental vegan food.
Ramona cuts a pig in half.
they eat in silence

They eat in silence until
he strips naked
Ramona says, "no avocado for you"
rumi says, "ni pa' los gabachos"
and cries into a bowl of grapes through tears

Ramona opens a cookbook,
turns to page 42
grabs two large eggs
½ a teaspoon of parsley flakes
one teaspoon of grated cheese
oyster mushrooms, Japanese bread crumbs
mild olive oil, kosher salt
and Aioli made with plum tomatoes.

rumi walks in with a newspaper in hand,
his beard covered in crumbs
& the scent of garbanzos

RAMONA'S INSTRUCTIONS ON HOW TO HANDLE THE DEATH OF A PET CHICKEN

On how to handle the death of a pet chicken:

get down to her level, look into her eyes,
promise her she won't be eaten, tell her she's
the prettiest chicken that ever lived,
read a poem about clouds to her,
code-switch when praying at her feet,
show her where her altar will be when she passes,
bring the other pets in the family to show respect,
promise you won't eat eggs for nine days as a novena,
kiss her beak, and wait.

Ramona sings her a lullaby,
rumi at a distance, shovel in hand,
prays to the earth for permission to dig.

RUMI'S INSTRUCTIONS ON KISSING BEFORE ANYTHING ELSE

Get nervous.
Let your palms sweat.
Don't confuse the stirring in your stomach with a bad meal.
Smile.

Go from tender to savage in a second
Return to tender.

Meet in a dark place.
In a car.
Listen to music.
Wait for the right lyric.
Reach out for her hand.
Always look into her eyes.
Always.

Tell her she's gorgeous.
Don't stop looking into her eyes.
Even when she adjusts her blouse and looks down.
Look at her hands.

Thumb away at her fingertips.
Stay tender.
Meet her halfway.
Kiss her like appreciating a piece of art.
Let her lips whisper what she wants.
Listen to her sighs between kissing.

Put your palm on her face.
Breathe.
Tell her lips.
Everything you want them to know.

WAKING UP IN AUGUST

rumi fights to wake,
the sheets all but on the floor

He dreams of torches
& chants of "No Border Walls"

Ramona counts the
crumbs of broken bread

She sweeps the summer heat
with a love song

rumi wakes and meets her in the kitchen
says, *you won't believe the dream I had*

Ramona hands him the paper,
I believe every single nightmare of it.

rumi levitates in the middle of the room

Ramona makes a call and starts preparing
for the visit from her witches

EVENINGSONG

Ramona is burning
rumi meditates on the small
of her back, kissing her hurts
she's still in flames

Spring arrived and a new moon
delivers an eveningsong
one in the morning and the birds
on anacua trees whistle
back and forth
mating calls,
dog's howl a suffering
canto into the night

rumi's hands have grown,
covering Ramona's body
she's still on fire
he knows what to do
opens his mouth
a song emerges

It's him vs la luna
eveningsong vs luz de madre
the moon perishes

Ramona is in ashes
rumi blows her remains
into the the empty sky

A SNACK BEFORE DYING

Ramona hands rumi a sharp object,
rumi peels an apple, feeds it to her blindly
& plucks on the tendons in his right arm

She sings a solemn tune

The table is set
cheese and wine from Chile

rumi drinks
Ramona waits
in the distance, a crow settles on a tomb

rumi reaches into his pants pocket
and pulls out a harmonica
blows deep lung songs
& listens to Ramona
moan with the cutting wind

rumi sits on the patio porch bench saying
goodbye to his last pack of cigarettes,

Ramona pours her first glass of whiskey
straight... neat.

EPILOGUE

Ramona grew old, very old.
spent some of her days on her stomach,
ear to the earth, listening for the many
souls of purgatory she prayed for daily
at 3 o'clock

She still takes her whiskey
straight, with a loaded gun
behind the bookshelf. She loved her
garden, there, she grew exotic
fruits and vegetables to feed
the orphans that snuck under
the lattice fence on the side of her home.
They never age, the children have
looked the same for years.
She never asked questions,
and they never spoke.

Nowadays, Ramona sleeps
like a tired lung, her dreams
are in slow motion.

rumi comes to her in dreams.

He slinks and follows her
footsteps in the sands of purple nights.
He's passed on
drawing her landscapes and pens
abstract love letters in the clouds.
He sends her wild winds and rains that
help in growing wildflowers.

Rumi, the cold front, the heatwave,
the retrograde, the supermoon,
the hightide, is constantly reminding her
of nature and a bigger presence, and the
best time of year to enjoy pomegranates and avocados.

He waits for her,
in no rush,
with a glass of whiskey and a cigar.

FROM

JAZZHOUSE, 2019

IN MY CITY

Trees sway a slow dance
To the leg song of the chicharra
To the long stretched acordeón
To the hiccups of 2am taco truck party-goers

Tlacauches maraud at midnight
With handy footwork across lawns
Grappling the humidity, eating away at
The molding bananas and lettuce offerings left out in a bowl
as a thank you for snacking on mosquitoes and cucarachas

Dogs bark at barking dogs that bark at wolf
moons and the incoming fog, at wobbly tire
passing cars, stray cats and late night chatter
from insomnia stricken artists burning the midnight oil

I pass by a home with a chandelier hanging from a branch,
another with a year round yard sale, and several with red doors
with scattered leaves from anacua trees confettied across their lawns

The people in this city move about like ants,
carrying the weight of life and hard work,
grackles stretch their song in long verses like the summers here,
I set my car on cruise control over the expressway and park
on a lot to see airplanes descend while scraping the syrup
top off my chamoyada raspa

I look at my phone and my friend just posted another
photo of palm trees under the hashtag #rgvpalmas,
On Sundays we choose barbacoa or tamales
Or Menudo for the cruda after being rattled awake by the
neighbor's lawn mower

I've been stretching my bones across the RGV,
from San Benito to Mission and in between
But longed to settle in McAllen, where my poems
Found their muse, and my dog ages at my feet.

IN LOVE WITH

our house
and the wood flooring
the creaking under my bare feet
and my walk over to the kitchen for a glass of water
All leading back to you

In love with the bending hiss of the cat
and their hideout: the broom closet.
Our cookbooks that opt out of my favorite dish: pupusas revueltas
and the motion in the king size bed
All leading back to you

In love with her music choices
the sound of faint trumpet sounds
melancholic piano suicides that are given second chances
and our future flower beds, tree swing, winter storms and child
All leading back to you

In love with gossip
and the mystery behind the words
the truth behind the lies
and the cutting of ties and relief
All leading back to you

In love with colors
the way our bedroom becomes an ocean
and our living room becomes a cliff overlooking the city
and our windows let the light in
All leading back to you

TONIGHT IS THE NIGHT

She said, Tonight, I'll be your chola
Shadows her eyes a drive-by purple
While chalk outlines her lips
she colors them blood red... on purpose
Lowrider oldies escaped through
The gap from my driver's side window
Letting out rings of humo
from my frajo and her yesca
I swerved while taking
Narcissistic selfies over the caliche road
Bearing a family of crosses
Some large, a few too small to accept
Spitting sunflower seeds into cotton fields
I sang to my spur-of-the-moment chola
As she finished off her look
tilting a fedora over her lowrider eyes
She looked over at me for approval
I nodded, like saying simon
Leaned over and kissed her shoulder
Daddy's Home came on and I sang
Along while the sombrero shaped cloud
Morphed to hearts, elephants, and a child
waving goodbye

INSTRUCTIONS

Cortázar gave me instructions
on how to beat insomnia, on the first night...

read to the moon for 10 minutes,
read to a cat for 9,
the dog 8,
a child 7,
a stranger 6,
a doll 5,
a painting 4,
a book 3,
my feet 2,
my hands 1,

and if I'm still awake, write to each, a letter of

apology.

JAZzHOUSE

I.
I tossed my copy of China Cowboy inside
my 9 year-old's bathtub basket, spilling her conditioner
made for rebellious hair. I need to remember to get it out
before she reads it. Before she asks,
"Why can't girls with flat faces be cowgirls?"

II.
I waited for her to return home. I sat and wrote
a letter to God. I tore it up and wrote it again.
Tore it again. When she came home, she was in tears.
I wondered if she felt his last breath inside
before the forceps grabbed on.

III.
I sat drinking coffee. Dipped the pan dulce,
losing some of it to the bottom of the chicory blend.
I need instructions on how to bleed right.
I need to know this before I put my bones out for sale.

IV.
I saw a coquí frog swallow
a little girl whole, a trumpet cry into
an alley being followed by pieces of children,
toes and hearts, cancer waiting in line for meds,

I saw a woman knitting herself a hand with her feet,
a storm approached and as it neared my heart filled with love,
it was her violent   jazzy voice.

DIEZ

1. My mother's hands smell of minimum wage pan dulce

2. Breakfast costs $2.25 before 11 am, no one should be starving between 7 and 11

3. My brother's eyes are borrowed pools of ocean water

4. My gums are losing your flavor

5. I've replaced her eyes with a garden, uprooted

6. Sometimes I'm asked to chop parsley, real fine

7. Roll call: grackles, widows, poets, glass cutters, and mannequin makers.

8. My dad saw a light, he ran to it

9. Solitude, thank you Duke Ellington

10. Bring a beehive to my funeral, tell them all about it.

CITY OF GOD

I woke up with the weight of my beard across my body. It had grown down to my feet. It was thick and coarse. There were people living on it. From the braid on my chest I could smell the food they were cooking. Down by my waist, my beard had the shape of hills with goats and other animals running around. I saw giants by my ankles, gentle and helping little people move up from the sheets by my feet. I sneezed and lost a race of people to the right side of my knees, where down below my cat ate them all. Quickly from my mouth emerged millions of babies that crawled to the open land where those same people fell off. By afternoon a city was built and by nightfall the violence began. I closed my eyes and a darkness fell over them all. In my slumber I could hear cries, moans and whispers of bad intentions. If this continues, I will shave in the morning, keeping only a mustache where across my lips dwell a goddess and a man.

I WISH YOU

Magic and love
Empanadas y aguas frescas
Sunsets and spices
Cold fronts and hot soups
Abrazos y besos
Fireworks and new colors
Tears of joy and friendships
Babies and pets and art and poems
Health and strength
Vacations and couch cuddles
Long walks and long baths
Long kisses and long days off
Inspiration and musings
Resolutions that last and water
Dancing feet and shower singing
Flowers in your garden and bees
Poems again. Poems again.
Barefoot walks in your yard
Rain dances and the moon
Coffee and Jazz, especially
Jazz

ODE TO THE SHAPE OF THE CAT'S HISS

Zip, Zig-Zag, dash
      You yank the air with you,
Across the green tiled floor
      Resting on the window sill

Bird gazer,
      Thinking of ways to
Feast upon the rooster's song in one pounce

You throw yourself at the moon
      Like a ninety-eight mile per hour pitch
After growing the batter tired of breaking balls

Architect of nighttime shenanigans
      tango with insomnia
Pencil in dark alleyway sexcapades

Hiss, scratch, bend
      The shape of your voice
When the door knob turns at midnight

PANDEMIA & OTHER POEMS, 2020

GOD IS

I

God is an open wound. A kung-fu movie and a celestial sicario.
God made our president with leftover road cotton and grackle
droppings. His sandals are of leftover human skin from the
factory of suicide rock stars, today he wears the knee caps of Janis
to match his ufo belt. God is unfazed at 3pm. He whispers to me
from a six feet distance. God lays naked on steel surfaces with his
long hair covering the shadow of men. God has a sticker on his
chest that reads "I voted."

He's nonchalant. He has a twin. She does all the good work.

II

God is your gods God, yoga and breathing, she is the breath of
life, latex gloves and exhaling the sun over mountains, she is
the blamed, the curve, the torn achilles heel, God is a beat poet,
the coming strain, the big question, the control, the last minute
mind changer, the finger on the gun, the safety switch, God is the
ultimate filter, the event planner, the street cleaner, the thing in
the sky that was there and then was not, the ventilator, the death toll.

She knows the bodies are coming.

III

God is language, a lisp and stutter, God has down syndrome, the
autistic genius, the only child, from the other side of the tracks,
have you ever thought of God as old? The wrinkled hobo and
toothless smoker, the girl next door, the square-jawed bad

hombre, creator of a new earth between ellipses, growing peonies on hyphens, god is soil and water. The trans angel, the monk making booze, the anorexic gargoyle breaking off a ledge, the movement in the painting, God's number is eight digits behind iron bars, the noise maker, the vuvuzela in purgatory, guilty!

God is doing time.

IV

God is a found poem, in exile, an unbelievable truth, an asteroid belt crash, mammoth, THAT sound, THAT silence.

V

G o d is tired of rising on Easter. G o d is trying to figure out the diameter of this pandemic, writing ghostly hymns for the dead. Did you not know G o d was the celestial laureate? Skywritings, the sounds you hear in the morning, of birds and wind chimes, speeding cars and barking dogs, did you think the sound was just that? Commotion? G o d writes those sounds into existence everyday. I know when G o d is in a Motown mood, a hippie rock or just a lounging jazz mood, and when it's too quiet... G o d let the whiskey get the better of him.

VI

God likes to drink with me. I listen.

LOS PÁJAROS SABEN

Los pájaros saben
>They perch on wires looking down at me with sorrow

Los pájaros saben
>I whistle a tune, the kiskadee turns away

Los pájaros saben
>the moon is sliced in half, beyond the western skies

Los pájaros saben
>The mockingbird's orchestrate, the shrill of a pandemic

Los pájaros saben
>the woodpecker's morse code is the answer

Los pájaros saben
>the nervousness in the way my wrists toss bird seed

Los pájaros saben
>They know of the dying clergymen in Italy & locusts in Oman

Los pájaros saben
>Why the river feels so familiar to drowning children

Los pájaros saben
>That a poet stands below them in search of words

IMAGES

The pandemic gave me a chance to see the wind and its curves
and laces as she glides through me

Jazz gave me a dirty look

Spring is here and there is no Monday thru Friday and Sunday is
Friday and Saturday died

My mother knits with her sister and are aging together with love
and remembrance

The mockingbird is learning a new flight pattern to go with her
new song

Children sit in tent cities, still, still

Doctors and nurses are rockstars, when can we say rockstars are
doctors and nurses

I'm afraid, yet I work through these ghostly streets of uncertainty

GENERATION Z

they both stare at their phones
kid tugs at dad's shirt
then mother's dress
neither budge
kid sits on floor, picks up a snake
eats the snake, then throws up
kid stands up, begs for attention
sits back down, picks up a gun
puts gun in mouth, pulls the trigger
parents stare at each other
get on their phone, download an app
to give them instructions on how to cry

TODAY I SALUTE THE HOMELESS

For his slow walk in this Texas inferno
In deep thought
Because anguish cripples our speech
At times, clenches all openings

I salute his hands
His black nails and ashy fists
His cracked wrists that look
as if they'll fall off if given a handshake

I salute her face
The history in her eyes
The forgotten kisses on her lips
The hills of his nose
The cheeks a mother once adored
The experience of a country's burden

I salute his legs
Her untracked miles
His chiseled calves
Her broken knees of prayer

I salute her heart
His home
Her love
His safegarden
Her hope
His wealth
Her family
His thankfulness
Her beat, all pumping in song

I salute the homeless, with a sign, with a smile, with a cup, with a moment, with a pause, with my time, with a truth, with an exchange, with an understanding, that maybe one day, I'll fall to my knees and ask Him to please forgive me for my sins and hope She can save me.

WHY ROSES LOSE THEIR FRAGRANCE IN AUTUMN

Because the planet curves
And you are my plum
I picked you from the apples
and peaches
and grapes
and every berry

Because you breeze through
like the fog and wrap your moisture on
deserving trees, let me be your oak and I promise
to house every singing bird on my highest branches

Because the sun is hazel today, and the ocean is birthing
fish for you to gather, and the moon waits
with her back turned to heaven, and each star
blinks its eyelashes for a long night of twinkling

Because the rooster wakes
at midnight preparing its throat
for the morning wake,
and the caterpillar of the giant leopard moth
struggles inch by inch in the dark,
and the dogs howl at passing shadows,
and every breath you take while you sleep is a question

Because I'm a prisoner in the veins of a poem,
and Elizabeth is sweating out her sins in a sauna,
and PW is committing poetry from coast to coast
from raging rivers in Colorado, to drowning rivers
In the Rio Grande and in between

Because she tells me to touch her soul
with sonnets, and her breasts
with tender strokes from my writing hand
and I boil water for coffee, and we listen to bootleg jazz,
and our naked souls dream with no eyes,
drinking water from the river of bodies forgotten,
and we die together daily, always at 5:55 pm
or just before the sun sets at the edge of the bay

Because "wow, you look so fish,"
and some fish don't act like real fish,
and David knows what I'm saying,
and love knows no gender, love is soul,
because love is respect
and kindness, and turtles crawl
out of their shell to run at night,
real fast, and flat-earthers hate cats,
and pussy willow grows
wild on the moon, and that is why
roses lose their fragrance in autumn

IF ROQUE DALTON WERE MY FATHER

I.
we would have discussions about the lake in the sky,
the longing for pupusas de loroco as we sit and fight off
the Texas heat drinking ensalada. I would be smoking and
he would be writing to El Salvador with his gray hands
(perhaps a poem, a song, a new anthem)
if Roque Dalton were my father, he too would have left me
and all i would have left
to remember him by would be
gunpowder, books
and that lake in the sky

II.
I would be his love
not the kind of love he's proud of
but the kind of love he suffers for

III.
We would sit in silence
we would crave it together, the halt of things
the respect for nature's song
the listening... for once
(not voices, sounds
Together, listening for the sound of pain
Together, searching for the place where it is adhered to)
No yelling
No screaming
No man made sounds
just our soles when walking

the crisp whispers of our clothes
when we slip into them
the sighs of the dying
and what of the marimba playing as we swallow black oysters?

IV.
Why do you pant?
your face tumbling downward, sinking into the ashes,
my heart.

I would ask about the birds and the bees,
How can anyone think of making love in this fire?

Son, everything burns
The streets
The walls
Our nakedness
Even the entrance to heaven

Sometimes we must not even look to the skies
Clouds want to go unseen when the bell tolls at noon

And we will sit in silence on the hillside watching the smoke
Listening to the sirens and gunfire, eating manguitos
trembling

V.
We have both lost
Good friends
Written their names in the sky
poured cold beer
On hot asphalt in their memory

I sometimes whistle when I think of the dead

JAZZISTA

What makes a Jazz poet?
not his shoes, not mine
bent to one side like a
matador waving a red
trapo en la cocina to
shoo-away las moscas
laying on the lip of my
taza de café con leche

(definitely not a grito!)

not writing a poem
during a cool docu
of Miles or Nina
talking in French
Bon Sang!

(an election is tweaked to
the sound of a trumpet solo) Now that zvuks like it sucks!

Órale! Cliché!
Even as a Latino youth
We be real cool but not too cool be be called a cuul -oh so we
stayed trucha, like
Coltrane and Tito
Arturo y Cachao
Bebo y Bobo

(stirring the beans
with Manteca de Gillespie)

JAZzistas live like cucarachas! They lay low and grab you by the huevos when you least expect it
when everything around you seems to be dying, the only thing louder than a bomb is the slow death of a JAZz sound A hard JAZz, an accusation, yeah A bop and hard 12-bar pandemic

SLEEPLESS IN PANDEMIA

I can't sleep much these   d a y s,
yet I'm tired and need to
I'm filled with strange   d r e a m s
that seem to be building a
  miniseries of   g r i m   realities at every turn

In the morning, I let out the dogs
there's a yellow   h a z e
that floats in my town
A stick-to-your   s k i n
enfermedad

This   p a n d e m i c   has me
thinking,
Is there a   g o d?
then I remember the stories
the poetry and prose of the
antepasados, the   f a i t h of my abuela
the observation of nature's language

And   I b r e a t h e   in place
P a n d e m i a   V i r u s

We seem to be more together in this

                                        distance

This morning, the first flock of loros

made their way to the wires
above our house

C a n t a n d o

A grackle perched,

head lowered   at a   distance

THIS IS HOW YOU DISMANTLE GRIEF

here I am writing poems again
joy has left my side for a bit
now I need to write about it
to remember the feeling

don't tell me to describe the shape of
ominous clouds anymore
I won't look up

I won't look at the moon
the stars, well... they were never really there
not like hope

every woman is you and not you
every song is playing tricks on me and
delivering the blues

I see flowers,
they're still a reminder of my
love for you, a warmth

I was blaming you and coffee
and nature and poetry
and God

this is how you dismantle grief
this is how heart's cry
this is me saying, forgive me
this is me saying, I love you
this is me in your dreams, crying

RESTLESSNESS

I woke up
half man
half horse
a metamorphosis
an incomplete mist
laying on earth
looking up at clouds
making strange faces
waking birds at dawn
feeling my heart
pump bloodheat
to my tired
lung

I WOKE UP

I woke up and realized they took away my language, Mother. I wanted to call you but I couldn't understand the operator so she hung up on me. I dialed again and my tongue got stuck to my cheek like a key on a typewriter, and she hung up again. I had been asleep for over two years, so I decided to write to you, now mother, understand that when I say they took away my language I mean it, I hope you find a translator, I found a piece of paper near my bedside that read, "your mother has been deported back to her shithole country" whatever that means, but there was also an envelope here with a return envelope with your name and a bunch of numbers of what seemed to be a group apartment or complex. Anyways, I hope you get this and I hear from you soon, I love you and let me know what happened.

YOU CAN'T BE A WRITER AND HATE TREES

not even if one falls on you or kills someone you love.
Do clouds feel the pain when they tear apart from each other?
What is the sound of their grief?
Which holds the rain and which morphs into
an elephant with a knife through the heart?
Which one heads to the mountain head on?
And which one loves the most?
Do they make sounds when they dissipate?
What of their gray throats?
Does the sun pierce through the oldest?
Does the moon have any use for clouds?

There's a mild chatter
the rain gives on these iron
stairs that lead to you
It rained and then it didn't
My smile lasted longer

Do my hands run across your body like a train hugging
its tracks heading strong into a dark tunnel to die without fear?
 Or do they feel like rain, my sweet flower?

There's a town
where the dead live parallel to each other
above ground in homes with sad eyes,
there are also those dead that live blocks away
just a few feet under, with life to spare

New York, did Lorca write your story?
Did he walk into your city like a skyscraper
with legs writing on you like a graffiti artist

in the forgotten hours of night?
Does he dare to write about my bordertown with truth?
Does his duende walk along the banks of the Río Grande,
weeping?

Has anyone bothered to ask the trees for the truth?

MIRASOLES

They said they're tearing down all the sunflowers, my love My love,
they said they're tearing down all the sunflowers

In their place, milkweed

                          milkweed, in their place

The monarchs are gliding over rivers, their caterpillars need it for
survival They want to plant sunflowers on the moon, my love

My love, they said the moon will be full of sunflowers

They will send a grackle or two to make sure they grow, my love My
love, there's going to be a moon full of grackles

The moon will turn black, my love
My love, the sky will be dark

There will be a squawking coming from the heavens, my love

I will plant sunflowers in your garden, my love, I will plant them
tomorrow Tomorrow, near your tombstone

                          I will plant sunflowers

THE MORNING AFTER

In the news
the lungs of the
earth are ablaze

I lay my head back
another day, my pillow
is on the floor

I stretch...
look at my hands
and my left thumb is
still trembling

I walk outside
fill the basin with water and listen to the birds gossip
on branches above me

I talk to them
I feed them
I wait and watch,
the mockingbird is
the first to drink

I go back inside
run the water until it warms the man in the mirror
waits for my next move We both stare

It's quiet
throughout the home
a light snore escapes my daughter's partially
opened mouth

I kiss her forehead
and tell her I love her

There's no coffee again just a meow from behind
saying "I'll be here
when you get back"

I drive off
stop to buy a
pack of gum
and cigarettes
coffee and the paper

Maybe today
is the day to write
a poem for autumn

That's as cool as
I can get nowadays
I can barely make a fist on days like this
and sometimes...
that's as cool as I want to be

FROM

CRY, HOWL, 2022

READING ON THE RTD, 1991-1993

Before I had a car
I read on the bus to and from work
I read Black Boy and Native Son
I read Invisible Man and Always Running
I read Dostoyevsky and some Langston Hughes
I read the L.A. Times and the Herald Examiner
I read many books and magazines
But mostly, I read the graffiti on the bus
& the faces of the beat, of the nervous
I read the lines on their hands & scars on their faces
I read the abuse and hungry and scared
I read the beauty on the eyeshadow and contour
on womens faces, the miles on their heels
I read the eyes of the drunk and heartbroken
I read their shoes for their travels and aches
I read their breath, the long sighs and whispers
I read on the RTD bus line
& now... I will write about it.

ROBBED AT KNIFE-POINT

The bus ride was bumpy and too fast,
it was definitely a weekday
I always walked to the back of the bus,
window seat facing the right side
where I could see the people get on and off

I could see the gutters, the businesses opening up early,
the drama of the day unfolding, lovers holding hands, stray dogs
panting and rummaging through trash, the homelessness of my city
extending their hands, my view was of the grind, la lucha.
I carried a backpack with books, cassette tapes,
and markers for taggin' even though
I sucked at it and had given up on it
several years back, It was a constant for me

That day I jumped on the bus on 7th & Spring,
I remember I was listening to some Roger & Zapp,
I was a bit tired from the double shift
I worked the day before. Between songs and reading
from Rodriguez' "Always Running" I heard voices,

grunts, and the sound of people pushing against
each other as the bus filled up. I scooted my body
and leaned my head on the graffiti marked window,
then dozed off.

My eyes opened up a bit later to see a short,
long-haired kid, white t-shirt, and Dickies pants,
Nike shoes, pinche cholo cagao'
I dressed the same in my barrio.

He kept looking around, hands in pockets
as if he were cold. The bus came to a stop
near McArthur Park, want to see a melting pot?

If you didn't get shot, stabbed, or drowned in
the lake there, you were fortunate. That day
I got robbed at knife-point.

This is what I remember: The bus stopped, people were getting
on and off and this kid in his teens pulled out a knife and stuck it
to my neck with one hand while he took my watch and backpack,
with the other, jumped off the bus and walked away.

The bus driver never saw it, and no one made a commotion,
I looked at him run away with my bag, inside
the pages of Ellison and Villaseñor
became instant orphans.

The bus slowly pulled away,
I stared at the lake, a lone swan sat on its murky waters,
I hadn't seen a swan so beautiful as that one, and haven't since.

CRY, HOWL

I

In your morning fog yawning at
daybreak

I feel your
suck and moan
in letters

Steal me an avocado from the grocery
store or ask father
he gives them away for free

Cry
when she cries
when she cries
Cry

Howl
as you die
as you die
Howl

Cry
for my city
running on warning
& low wattage
on low wages
& melting asphalt

Howl
In your pastel
queer dreams

& flip flops
from the top
of the stairs
& heroin blasted toes

Cry, Howl
On Juneteenth
for the real beat lyrics
of Amiri, Kaufman, & LeRoi

Cry, Howl
the disappearance of
privilege and the ugly squads the sinking
of ships carrying
Conservative literature printed in China
for the hypocrisy

Cry
when she cries
when she cries
Cry

Howl
as you die
as you die
Howl

Cry, Howl
for Lawrence
& Jim Morrison

& Robert & Bob
& Roque & Francisco
for the new strain
for the math in pandemia

To our dead
For you we cry
For you we howl
For you we drink
For you we eat
For you we kill
For you we harvest
For you we work
For you we develop

Howl
here come the UFOs
here come the blamed
here come the white teeth
Nothing has changed
The avocado seed sprouts a root

Howl
like the quarantine dogs
the shuffling winds from the east like the wailing
orchestra of orphans like a city under water,
moonless

Cry
for the absence of music
for the spilt milk
for the herniated disc along the border for its water

Cry
when she cries

when she cries
Cry

Howl
for the ghetto girls
for the bass in your face
for January 6th pardons
for strange fruit

for boycotted fruit
for books

Howl
as you die
as you die
Howl

To the new administration
pick a nation
Bitcoin buys me pupusas
but don't come here
we'll send your ass back
put the beast on reverse
coffins on high demand
pipelines shut down
sacred land spared, for now

Cry
Into the river
Howl
Between the mountains cleavage
Into the dead eyes of lonely streets

Howl, Cry
On the perfect canvas of oil paint

Take the spirit of the steed
Shoot your bullets up to the clouds Morph them into
stretched veins

II

Ain't no big thing
Nationwide shortage of
Chicken wings

Someone is crying into the phone of gluttony

III

Cry,
For the smell of age
Howl
& blot out my rebellion

IV

My skin tags play a game of
hide and seek when I sleep
My nose bleeds when
I get horny and fussy
I drip poets into the drain of murals
Into the drain of obscurity

V

Cry, Howl

I still love the way your voice spreads like cream
When the hummingbird sucks on spoiled nectar &
how the earth is crashing down into a merlot hue

while Whitey sits on the moon
& I don't know why
We mistook our tears for water

Howl
as we climb the tree that thrives on loneliness Cry
when we get to the top and find a rope

VI

Cry,
When you don't make it

Howl,
Where all the dead lie
Make a revolution with fire and blood Especially if
the dead are
children

RIO GRANDE, RIO BRAVO

I hear your whispers,
it's not the wind speaking anymore
it's your longing and your spirit
in the leaves, in the ripples, in the razor teeth of separation
Entre tierra mojada, the scent of mud
that brings me to you, the birdsong that makes its way to us from
across two lands that share the same language of the heart that
brings me to you
Rio Grande, Rio Bravo
the hope of a new people
the baptism of the new mestiza, nepantlera
We hear the echoes of pain and struggle and
the chants of "si de puede! y aquí nos quedamos"
Rio Grande, Rio Bravo
it's not the wind speaking anymore
it's the water
it's the water
it's not the wind speaking anymore
Rio Grande, Rio Bravo
we hear the echoes of pain and struggle and
the chants of "si de puede! y aquí nos quedamos"
the hope of a new people
the baptism of the new mestiza, nepantlera

Rio Grande, Rio Bravo
entre tierra mojada, the scent of mud
that brings me to you, the birdsong that makes its way to us from
across two lands that share the same language of the heart that
brings me to you,

it's not the wind speaking anymore
it's your longing and your spirit
in the leaves, in the ripples, in the razor teeth of separation I hear
your whispers

GOD AS TREE, TREE AS GOD

"If the rumble of the remote
tree disturbs you
it is not for lack of concern."
—Tezozomoc

I sometimes think god is in the trees
my tree especially, god is my tree

the birds that hover over His crown, angels
who bring petitions and offerings from the four directions

god, is the sun and moon to the ancestors
the eternal dreamers preparing the way

god, is the veins of mother earth
the roots, the rocks, the soil, the witness

I lay my hands on my god when I am fatigued I lay my cheek on
my god when I need an answer I place my lips on my god when I
am thankful I sit at god's feet when I need a friend
I place my hands on my god when I'm losing faith

I sometimes think my god is in the trees
my tree, the trees I drive past, the trees on tv
burning by the thousands, the ones falling alone in the forest the
new ones being planted, uprooted

my god in the trees
breathing slowly, not complaining
breathing harder, transforming

breathing, liberating themselves from sin
breathing, unifying nature
breathing, for the resurrection

my god, my life, tree

MAMA'S STRUGGLE

Mama always dressed for comfort.
The hardest part was getting undressed.

The tucking of large breasts into a cheaply
made bra that by the end of the day left deep

creases over her shoulders and along her sides.
Sometimes she would ask one of her sons to help

her with the strap and connect the little eye hooks.
Mama's body had scars.

A simple article of clothing: fabric, foam cups, sliders
rings, hooks, and underwires.

Mama never complained, she patted the cuts with
alcohol swabs and ointment.

Mama had one bra and many scars.

CAPSIZED

a poem about alcoholism

I always thought of dad as an ocean
spume frothing from his mouth

mom would say tilt his head to one side
I pretended I controlled the sea

somewhere waves were created when I did that
so I looked at him and drew tiny boats on

his lips and cheeks, he moaned and groaned and I
pretended the sea was mad, so I drew

pirates on his chin, sometimes the sea would
gargle and toss back at me all the plastics and

garbage, pieces of sailors and forgotten
ships would emerge, one time he opened his eyes

and his green orbs flashed a mermaid
playing a violin, playing a song of longing

AUTUMN 2016

The little girl with amber hair first came to me in the fall of 1989. She sat with her back against me not too far from the pile of fire ants that aggravated me every day. I remember she had this large pink bow in her hair, Mary Jane shoes, and a small plush doll that always rested between her right underarm. She was an only child. Her parents were separated by alcohol and domestic violence and finally... too many sleeping pills. She lived with her grandmother in the house that sits on one and a half acres, about twenty skips away, if you have long legs. Something about trees that humans find good use for, piñatas on birthdays, a large tire for swinging, carving out their love's initials, sticking fire crackers in my tiny holes, climbing (which I don't mind at all) and like the young girl, someone to cry and speak to.

Just about a foot away lies buried the family dog. He was old and sick and was put to sleep. She cried and visited him often. I saw her grow and she stayed loyal to me. Especially in the fall. This is when she laid near me on a blanket and stared at the sky for what seemed like hours and hours. She cried and wrote in a journal and had her first kiss on the other side of me, where the woodpecker left a decent hole for her to stick notes in. She was only 16 in the autumn month of November when she had her first kiss. The boy was afraid and so was she. He had tamed hair, black, with a sharp chin and brown skin. Her eyes were like my leaves, an orange and light brown hue of early December.

I never saw much of the rest of the family, they gathered in the living room and kitchen, or sat up front with the ash trees. There, the squirrels chased each other for long sessions and all I could hear were the rustling of leaves and branches and the occasional giggle from the adults smoking marijuana, and listening to Tejano music. She was the only friend to my looming branches that gave the impression of wanting to be grabbed and broken off. She didn't do that though, she caressed my leaves and appreciated my shade.

Late September of 2016, she came to me at 3am. I felt something graze my branches several times before I felt a pull and a nervous hurrying motion. Then a long weight came down on me. God blinded me. All I could do was make out muffled sounds. In the morning the sun's heat put me to sleep. Over the years I have discovered that that is what happens to us when human tragedy and nature come together.

Her name was Autumn.

IN THE CEMETERY

A tombstone — a sorrowful gray
there lies a poet
his only visitors — pigeons
the occasional writer with
a pad and pencil
conjuring inspiration from the grave
a child — the birthday flowers
& tears of remembrance
the friend — reads new poems
from an anthology of odes to rust

      Carved granite
      Slowly becoming a memory
      but did the poet not write about this?
      the grave — death — obscurities ?

The undertaker — listens
walks with a slow wither
that's what feeding grackles will do to pensive man
lost in his slow walk — like a stray bullet

      Mounds of marble — teeth of the city
      sinking into the gums of the earth
      cavities of silence
      the narrow lips of father
      the knuckles of abuelita
      the dead suit of abuelo
      the four winds of pandemia

In the cemetery:
Curtains — drawn down
everyday is a celebration of life

time passes — nothing changes
music comes in the form of footsteps and moans

flowers are pushed up for the living — flowers are pushed up, for
our grief

I RETURN TO LOVE L.A.

We landed on time. The pavement outside
the small airplane window was wet, and from where I sat
I could almost smell the petrichor
settling in
on la la land.

I've missed my city, a mourning at times
The smog   The homelessness   The crime
The struggle, All of it!
The cholos and cholas The low riders
Whittier Boulevard,
City Hall and all its suited criminals,
the immigrant culture, the graffiti,
the ghetto bird, the flat foots, the taggers, the pinche traffic jams,
the murals, the scent of gunpowder... sadly, hasta eso!
the second I step foot
the streets gave me the chisme,
on the corner of hustle

I saw raw courage and fight in a school teacher
holding up a strike sign! Oh yeah! She was like
the Statue of Liberty, like a Virgencita Guadalupana,
como una flor, la Emma González, la Alexandria Ocasio-Cortez,
asi mero!
She smiled for my camera and continued her grito,
on the corner of Mission and Yellow Caution Tape Boulevard

My mother, hit seventy years of age
and still dances on Wednesday afternoon,
my chiquita viejita, always busy, still making

the best coffee and desayunos, I stare at her
watching a soccer match on television,
I can almost feel my dad next to her,
he left his costumbres for her to carry,
she misses him,
the flat on Gabriel Garcia Marquez knows it
Some things have changed and some stay the same:
They've moved my gente con gentrification,
the mariachis are still hustling on Boyle
strumming and tuning their guitarrones,
the borrachitos are still stumbling in and out
of the bar with the velvet curtain
except it's now a puerta de madera,
there on la calle primera

On the corner of shank and choke
Are the huddled men that lost hope
Fists closed around a bottle of memory
Glossy eyes not to be mistaken with tear welling eyes,
glossy... like distance.
The fathers of the barrio, the forgotten ones,
the addicted ones, the lost ones across Hollenbeck Lake

Across from wounds and addiction
Are the women that were robbed
Hair chopped short with blue-veined breasts that leak earthmilk,
long fingernails to climb and detach tomorrow's suicides,
the women of wounds, raising children,
goddamned children of the barrios, birthing more
children in safe zones, trying to rush into
menopause and divorce, slicing the bully in
the gut, breaking away from the man, breaking away
from the plan that the man can with no plan.

I return to love L.A.
Introduce her to my daughter

whose hazel eyes are like a California sunset,
whose skin is bronze by ancestral blessings,
whose voice code switches with the morning whistling
of Santa Ana winds, who's morning yawn stretches
from Tejas to el Centro de Los Ángeles

I return and love my L.A.
with a new set of eyes, translating poems in
the shape of birds on power lines and river water
under the bridge, on the tracks,
where boxed cars wait to be pushed across the country,
Where homeless women push
shopping carts filled with garbage stanzas,
leaving poems in my mother's palms,
where palm trees sway with morning traffic,
I throw my city poems out the window
driving on the 5 and pause to breathe
on the 10 heading west

Until I return, I will hold my breath
I will hold it long enough
To remember
I never left

ELEGY FOR VANESSA GUILLEN

You disappeared in the spring, bluebonnet
They found you in the summer

robbed of your privacy
taken at the tender age of twenty

I never liked camouflage, but when
I see your photo on social media, the news
now on murals, I respect it, for you

A guerrera, una hija, a voice silenced

I go to my tool box
throw my hammer across the room
turn off the commercial with
4th of July advertisement
and hate camo again

You disappeared in the spring, sunflower
They found you in the summer

If we say your name enough times
Will you respond? maybe in the shrill
of the thirsty mockingbird in my garden

You are in the wind, like my father
like our friends taken in this pandemic,

O Specialist,

Dug deep with the lies,
America's daughter

You disappeared in the spring, lilac
You were found in the summer
Missing the dark skin of your ancestry

A secret unmasked by the thunder
of a mother in mourning of the riding voices
still chanting their echoes of justice

After the first death, there is no other
And yet, here we are again

You went missing in the spring, soldier
Your song was found in the summer

Maybe soon, they'll raise your
name to honor a school,
a park, a highway, an airport

Maybe sometime in spring
when flowers bloom wildly along
the highway, before another
dreaded Texas summer

NEW POEMS

WHAT IF JOY HARJO KNEW THE SECRET TO HEALING

What if Joy Harjo knew
the secret to healing
& horses carried all the poems
In their throats, songs of native lands

Songs
Songs
Songs

The river gropes
the ankles of running steed

If a horse looks up to the sky
what forgiveness does it seek

As a child I wondered
what language was spoken through
their neigh, what music slices
through their hooves

A man painted horses in
reds and purples
the man set the stallions
against a New Mexico sunset
Is this what Joy Harjo meant of
them cutting into the edge of the sky

What strength
What speed

What if they kept running

What if Joy Harjo knew
the secret to healing
& horses carried all the poems
In their throats, songs of native lands

Songs
Songs
Songs
You can never bury the innocent
Sooner or later
Their blood will call

Sing
Sing
Scream through cheering greed

I stopped to watch glory in a brown body & a black mane
somewhere in between my move from California to Texas, I
was already feeling the heat of the border as it grazed quietly in
thought

What patience
What beauty
What eyes watching me cry

The man who painted horses moved to Honduras without the
color green
Now all his horses

Fly
Fly
Fly

RIVER

all the **women**
in my home
were bronze.
their skin
like **river** stones
out of water
slippery   Moon milk
Stars

Women.
Milk moon   **stars**
slippery
water out of
Stones, river like
their skin
bronze, were
home

all the women in my home were
Moon
River
Stars

MOONCHRIST

I watch the mummified drip
cream over, untouching lashes
spotlight on saguaro
pressing pollen deeper into earth's sinuses

show us the crypt
the sprouting hyacinth or
the simple rose

What's in the water? in the soul of rain?

So far
So alone
So profound
Yet, a mystery
Is there a razor in your throat?

What death did you have?

spotlight the peregrinos walking the stations
Is earth in your dreams?
Do you hear sounds?

Whispers?
I often think of your weeping
hanging there   aching
what sustains you,
glowing crucifix in the night sky?

I HAVEN'T BEEN TO CHURCH

since before the pandemic,
maybe even longer than that

I'm wearing my best, not a suit
my best, the brown shoes with laces

the button up shirt with a collar
& slacks with the shirt tucked in

the agua bendita once held by the gilt
is no longer available for my guilt

every bowl entering the Church
is dry, the bowl, as if aching

cracking, i swipe my fingers &
get nothing but dust and scratches

late as always, sliding across the back
wall looking for a place to sit

the looming eyes of St. Francis holding
a lamb, over my shoulder as I listen to

the congregation read from the screen,
"The Lord is my shepherd, I shall not want..."

I look around the pews & see the millionaires
saying it the loudest, we all want, we all want something
i think to myself, we all need something

& we sing, nevermind off-key, but sing our lies

the Church had a remodel, therefore a second
collection, I look at St. Francis and ask him for a dime

I could swear he smiled & the lamb bleated

WHEN DEATH COMES, & THE TREES WALK AWAY

You'll look at my dead body

Next to a dead book on a chapter or a poem somewhere in the middle of pages dog-eared on the left page, I'll be in a room with my dead black shorts and dead work socks, next to my dead cell phone and dead glasses, my dead toothbrush will still be wet and my dead razor will hold on to beard hair from my dead chin for another month after that, the deadest month

Half of our garden will leave with me, the dead cactus and dead roof with the dead shingles where the dead mockingbird will let out a dead song about living, amongst the dead

When death comes, schools will let out at the same time, traffic will jam, affairs will continue, love will love, and teenagers will fall in love, books will go unread and all of these things can make people sad, wish they were dead if it's for the last time, there's an accident, love turn to hate, hearts get broken, or books are banned

& I won't be here to see
the trees walk away from it all.

MORE WAITING

for my child to write her story

I tell her it'll help her find answers
But...

Her heartbeat drives her mad

Daddy, I just want to sleep
Daddy, I don't want to wake
Daddy, I don't know why I feel this way

I'm waiting
Her heartbeat is a million stars

I tell her avocados are still expensive but
I have faith that it's temporary
Like a toothache temporary
Like pain from when you stump a toe
Like rain in the forecast
Like a hummingbird between the eyes

In my dreams I walk

heartaches on-a leash and I walk with a hole in my head from
a wound from a prior dream/The scene is green, artichoke
green with brown waves on sandy shores, the ocean waves are
asparagus sticks and my child builds sandcastles with undertaker
shovels and black lipstick/melatonin vibrations/& a barge passes
by, blowing a trumpet signaling a red tide on the way/here come
the sharks/I'm looking for my child now/she's getting the knives
sharpened and strikes a match

In my dreams I sing

I call the sound saguaro & sangre de cusuco. I sing it long and soulfully, sans the blues & jazz. I pause to speak haiku lines and then wait for rain.

Wait
Wait
Wait

Her heartbeat is a rolling rock into a river

sounds different at 3am, I put my head to her chest and there's a skateboarder riding her veins doing slides and heelflips, nollies and grinds.

I'm waiting

For Billie Holiday to exit the subway & for Ginsberg to bring the sheets in from the clothesline. Hollywood actors I better not find out you don't like popcorn, or sticky floors at movie theaters or velvet curtains, I'm waiting for my trophy like all of you. My dreams end with curtain calls,
even when they see me with a hole in my
head & daisy seeds in my closed fists

I'm waiting

for the whole in the sky to release the turtle-necked apocalypse army angels with rainbow sashes to descend and take our jobs. Send the people that eat out & never tip to work the cabbage fields of Gunma. Send the male politicians with more than two terms to prison with permanent lip tattoos and eyelash extensions. Send the one term presidents to look up the rocket's ass at launch over at Boca Chica Boulevard. Send the street vendors glory. Send the gun owners self-kits on how to amputate their trigger fingers. Send a bouquet of Emory flowers to all women that have abortions.

Send me an angel,
Send me an angel

Right now
Right now

I WANT TO VISIT A PLACE WHERE LEAVES ARE BIGGER THAN MY FACE

I want to trip over branches and fall on these
brown & crunchy leaves

Stay in the ground laughing & smiling looking up to see
other leaves descending like tree stars

Green ones, more brown ones & the wind playfully tossing
them back up as I reach up to catch them

I'll be laughing, & at 48 years old forget that I tripped
& my ankle hurts and my shoulder too

I start to realize I've rolled over all the leaves & they no longer
make crunchy sounds & now I'm in the earth

& I see worms & ants & other bugs & I am not
laughing anymore, the wind is now silent and it's dark

The trees are looming over me with still branches,
holding their leaves & I, I am trying to laugh but I can't anymore

I'm just laying on my back, in the dark, on the earth,
waiting with the trees

Waiting for something to make me laugh again

SAGUARO

I had a dream that Esperanza Spalding came to town for a free concert. She opened the container to her upright bass and pulled out a saguaro that grew over ten feet over her head and bloomed white flowers. It was a spring concert. She plucked at the large cactus aggravating the spines to the start of the song "Cuerpo y Alma," Spalding played into the summer, ending the concert early due to bloody fingertips.

LULLABY OF THE PUPUSA

What love song in my mouth

Who smuggled in the chicharrón
between the curtido & Rosarios de abuela

Hermana de arepa y gorditas

El escándalo de loros entre mordida de loroco y queso
es nivel chulada, abuela would break her wrists to make it
leaving prints on the edges of the masa like a poem on a page

¿Dónde está la mara? los primos y amigos con las gaseosas
con la marimba, con las Regias, con los platanitos

Para que son buenos los dedos,
si no para doblar la pupusa

Round & thick
hot & gooey
as a kid, lived on
these pre-colonial frisbees

Cipota under the moon
smiling on a full tummy

Bichos en la finca modelo playing fútbol
take a break to talk about their
favorite filling before lunch

Pupusa, the two-time border-crosser

What love song in my mouth

Para que son buenos los dedos,
si no para doblar la pupusa

Y comer sabroso!

WHERE IS GINSBERG (ME VALE!)

"We're all golden sunflowers inside."
— allen ginsberg

In the avocado at the Valle Megamart / he's in the beard DNA oil sold at South Texas beauty supply near the black, blue hair dye cream / He's in the cup of elote con mayonesa, he's the mayonesa / & the tajin powder men lick up and down before guzzling their bud lights, they lick them bottles up and down, slow & / He's in the lechera at the raspa stand / On his way north on the greyhound.

Where is Ginsberg when not in soiled sheets? / He's down the drain

In the rain / In pain / smoking hash on the fire escapes of New York / He's in moans & menthol smoke / In a poet's pocket during Poem in Your Pocket Day / He's in the semen / The seamen are in him / In the sea of plastics & latex

He's in America / He's in the war protests / He's in the the shrieking of the chachalaca / He's in the Jesus pieces / & extra-large brown eggs /& potatoes

He's in currency / The zero-dollar bill / In machinery that doesn't work / mouth of plum blossoms / in the tar on my lungs

He's in techno music mucus / He's vomiting in San Diego at the zoo

/ He's beat / A whore banjo / A pack of incense / an amethyst rock

A fucking poet / He's in the trees / in the beads / in the anus / He lost a chancla / Y se murio/ y me vale!

ARRIVAL

By throat is how we arrived
A cradle in a voice
A passion & command

By hands is how we arrived
A touch
Skin rising, a cringing,
Churning of a bullet

By force is how we arrived
Scrapes and bruises
blood dripping & empty

By train is how we arrived
With prayer in our veins
With thirst & bloody lips
Trembling

By knife is how we arrived
A rip & tear
A cut & puncture
A sliced womb

By love is how we arrived
A fragrance & warmth
An acceptance, by chance

By death is how we arrived
A scalpel & trash bin
A plastic blanket lullaby
A rope

By miracle is how we arrived
A quiet river
A safe crossing
A push

ABOUT THE AUTHOR

Edward Vidaurre is an award-winning poet and author of eight collections of poetry. He is the 2018-2019 City of McAllen, Texas Poet Laureate, 2022 inductee to the Texas Institute of Letters, and publisher of FlowerSong Press. His writings have appeared in *The New York Times Magazine, The Texas Observer, Los Angeles Review of Books*, as well as other journals and anthologies. He has edited over 50 books and anthologies. Vidaurre resides in McAllen, Texas with his wife Liliana, their daughter Luisa Isabella, and their furry rescue babies.